RACE CAR LEGENDS

CHELSEA HOUSE PUBLISHERS

LOWRIDERS

Danny Parr ·

CHELSEA HOUSE PUBLISHERS
Philadelphia

Frontis: *T. J. Gutierrez of Velarde, New Mexico, transformed an ordinary 1949 Chevy pickup truck into an elegant lowrider. For owners like T. J., creating such works of art is an expression of themselves, their families, and their communities.*

Produced by
21st Century Publishing and Communications, Inc.
New York, New York
http://www.21cpc.com

CHELSEA HOUSE PUBLISHERS

Production Manager: Pamela Loos
Art Director: Sara Davis
Director of Photography: Judy L. Hasday
Managing Editor: James D. Gallagher
Senior Production Editor: J. Christopher Higgins
Publishing Coordinator/Project Editor: James McAvoy

The Chelsea House World Wide Web address is
http://www.chelseahouse.com

First Printing

1 3 5 7 9 8 6 4 2

Library of Congress Cataloging-in-Publication Data

Parr, Danny.
    Lowriders / Danny Parr.
        p.   cm.—(Race car legends)
    ISBN 0-7910-5849-2
    1. Lowriders—Juvenile literature. 2. Hobbyists—Juvenile literature. 3. Mexican Americans —Juvenile literature. [1. Lowriders. 2. Mexican Americans.] I. Title.
II. Series.

TL255.2.P37 2000
629.28'72—dc21

                                                                        00-031500
                                                                               CIP
                                                                                AC

CONTENTS

ONE OF A KIND

Perhaps you have seen a car or truck or van painted with brilliant colors or images. It probably rode on small wheels and was closer to the ground than a regular car. Such a vehicle is a kind of lowrider. "Lowrider" can have more than one definition, though. It can describe how people who are proud of their cars, trucks, or even bicycles make their vehicles special by customizing them. Lowrider might also refer to the owner or driver of a vehicle, or it can describe a set of wheels that its owners have hunkered down as close as possible to the ground. Most importantly, for those who create lowriders, their vehicles are an expression of their feelings about themselves and about others. For the Hispanic communities in California and the American Southwest, where the lowrider movement began, the vehicles are an expression of the people's love and respect for their heritage and traditions.

Lowriders, both the vehicles and their owners,

Whichever vehicle a lowrider chooses to create, it will be one of a kind. "Chantilly Lace," a 1950 Chevy Delux Fleetline, is one of 12 cars restored by Lawrence Griego of Albuquerque, New Mexico. Lawrence firmly believes that a lowrider is the expression of an owner's personality. "The nicer the car, the nicer the person," he says.

are one of a kind. Like the interstate highways that always seem to be in a state of rebuilding or renovating, a lowrider never stops changing its image. For the owners who cherish their vehicles, finishing their cars or bicycles (or even a model size of either) is not the plan. Instead, working on lowriders is a never-ending project, a lifetime hobby. The truck gets a new paint job or new, brighter rims. The car is rebuilt so it can jump higher or dance longer. The tricycle is dressed up as a showpiece that nobody rides. Whatever owners' imaginations can dream up, they apply to their wheels.

Like their vehicles, lowrider owners do not stay the same either. Changing something on their cars or trucks may be a signal that they too are changing inside. Seeing how special the lowrider undercarriage looks with chrome plating, owners may think about a habit or an attitude of theirs that needs spiffing up. Working on the lowrider with friends may be a way to learn about being patient with others. Older lowriders pass on to younger lowriders positive attitudes about habits and making choices, helping the younger ones to envision the kind of vehicle they want to create in the future. That is how the lowrider tradition lives on.

Many lowriders donate their time to encouraging young people to get off, and stay off, drugs or get away from, and stay away from, gangs. All of their work builds a lowrider reputation of honor and pride. To accomplish their mission, many lowriders devote their whole lives and their families' lives to being the best lowriders, passing on to others the knowledge of how to be the best too.

Of course, some drivers and owners have

their own personal reasons for being lowriders. Vincente Lujano likes his family to be involved in his drug prevention program as he works with students in middle and high schools. Tomas Martinez takes time from his job at Valley National Bank in Española, New Mexico, to promote the popularity of lowriders for families. Raul Tostado's lowrider vehicle honors the father he never knew.

A common objective among lowriders is to make an impression, to amaze spectators. How could what appears to be a pile of junk or weird scraps of metal end up being so strong and beautiful? onlookers ask with their eyes. Unmistakably, the products are

Xavier Nevarez and his son Fabian share the enjoyment of their 1977 Grand Prix. Closeness with family and community are all part of the lowrider tradition, which owners pass down from generation to generation.

Juan Dominguez of Chamisal loves to slowly cruise the back roads of New Mexico in his 1958 Chevy Impala. Where an owner drives is not as important as enjoying the time with his treasured vehicle and showing it off to others.

personal visions come true.

Sometimes the look of a lowrider dazzles because of outstanding artwork. Many owners treat their cars as canvases to display their favorite religious figures, while others paint tributes to family members in showy places on the vehicles. Some choose landscape scenes to honor their original homelands, and some have fun with snappy designs in bright colors that are sure to catch attention.

Imagine a hunkered-down car cruising quietly down the street. The driver pushes a switch. All of a sudden, the car jumps into the air like a bucking horse, slams back down on the road, and then slowly moves on its way again as if nothing happened. Passers-by scratch their heads and rub their eyes. Did I really see that, they ask themselves, or did I imagine it? The driver stares straight ahead, never cracking a smile. The action surprised the wondering viewers, just as the driver intended.

Other times, drivers are not satisfied with one hop. Instead, they guide their cars into jumping, knocking, and grinding between the road and an invisible marker high in the air. Their vehicles convulse up and down, move from side to side, or rock forward and back. To do these show-offy moves, a lowrider replaces the regular vehicle suspension systems with hydraulic cylinders and pumps. ("Hydraulic" means operating or moving an object by using pressure generated by water or some other liquid.) Some lowriders say the vehicle is not a true lowrider until it comes to life with hydraulics.

Displays of hydraulic action mostly take place at car shows, where owners have 90 seconds to demonstrate different moves and dances to win prizes. For example, the bed on Victor Garcia's truck, "Purple Haze," juts up high and dances in circles, tips from one side to another, and spins as fast as 35 mph. Tim Lona put hydraulics on his car, "The Wicked One," so that he can make the car leap high into the air. When Tim has made more changes, he will be able to force the wheels to leave the ground in pairs, or even three at a time, until the car has turned a complete circle—a move called Around the World.

Some cities have forbidden the use of hydraulics on regular roads and highways. Possibly, hopping vehicles interfered with traffic, or maybe the streets that once had a low traffic volume are now main thoroughfares. Or perhaps onlookers gawked at the lowriders and forgot to watch where they were going. The police claimed lowriders caused too much distraction and were dangerous with their tiny tires and chain-link steering wheels.

Lowriders were forced to find other places to show off their creations, and they did. The lowriders of New Mexico like the dirt back roads just fine. They can go where they want to and drive as slowly as they please. Parks and town squares are also great for cruising on Sunday afternoons in California. Giving the lowrider treasure some air and a little exercise matters more than the exact place where it is driven.

A true lowrider becomes a member of the family, is given a name, and is treasured as an heirloom. The vehicle represents the family history, the family members who helped create it, and symbolizes all the traditions and values that are important to the family. It is often handed down from one generation to another like a family portrait or a precious piece of jewelry. For Hispanic people, lowriders represent the stability of their culture, the ability of Hispanics to love, to be colorful, and to have fun. We treat our lowriders with respect and dignity, just as we want our families to be treated, Hispanics say.

Among the lowrider car clubs that have been formed, some honor this heritage by limiting their membership to Hispanics. Many car clubs, however, do not consider the ethnic background of their members. These clubs are aware that the lowrider movement has grown enough to appeal to anyone who likes to mess with a car in a lowrider way. Some clubs even have a policy that their membership must be a mixture of drivers from all different ethnic backgrounds. Steve Miller of Placentia, California, is the proud owner of a Euro lowrider, a real contest winner. He loves being a lowrider and is grateful that lowrider competition is open to people of all ethnic backgrounds.

As you will read in the pages that follow, a person of any age can be a lowrider. From children with tricycles, to their grandparents, who treasure heirlooms packed in crates for safekeeping, to those who make models of lowrider cars, trucks, bicycles, or tricycles, all have their reasons. They may keep their cars or trucks hidden and private, or they may show up at car shows regularly, hoping for a prize. However lowriders choose to treat their creations, their reasons are always personal.

CREATING A LOWRIDER

Wuhile a lowrider can start out as any kind of vehicle, the first step—perhaps the only agreed-upon requirement for making a unique creation—is lowering it close to the ground. After that, owners are limited only by their own imaginations. Sometimes owners envision the vehicle's look before buying it. Others may buy the wheels, study them, think about them, and check what others have done before settling on ideas that work for them.

The next most common change is a new paint job. Then owners might put on smaller wheels, add shiny chrome, and alter the doors, trunks, or hoods in some way. Once the owner has created the image he wants, he may sell the vehicle or, chances are, he will refashion it again and again. Either way, the owner has earned the name lowrider and has chosen a life-long interest that never ends.

It is possible that the all-important first step of lowering the vehicle was a way for the first lowriders

For Nicholas Herrera of El Rito, New Mexico, the remains of a 1939 Chevy were a challenge as he began remaking the parts into a lowrider. With imagination, skill, and a vision, lowriders can begin from scratch and turn a junked vehicle into a sleek, smooth set of wheels.

to get nearer to their roots. Perhaps they wanted to feel a connection with the earth. Even before anyone had figured out how to get cars down by altering their suspension systems, owners piled bags of sand or cement in the backs of their cars and trucks. Watching the trunks, fenders, and doors sag closer and closer to the ground, they liked what they saw.

By the 1950s, owners were experimenting with hydraulic systems to lower their vehicles. Some say the first hydraulics on a lowrider were built from surplus airplane parts; others remember hydraulic parts coming off delivery trucks. Today the most popular way to lower (and raise) lowriders is with cylinder hydraulics. Lowriders remove the springs and front shock absorbers from their vehicles and replace the shocks with cylinders connected to a hydraulic pump usually placed in the trunk of the car. Batteries power the pump to push fluid into the cylinders, which lift the vehicle's body. To lower the body, the driver flips a switch that uses the same pump to drain fluid from the cylinders.

Another way to change a suspension system is to torch or burn the coil springs on the wheels down to a lower position. This is a permanent change, and vehicles done this way are for cruising only. There are no high speeds, no bumps, no jumping, no messing around of any kind. Owners drive these lowriders slowly, show them off proudly, and carefully protect them. "This was the '50s way to make it low," Dennis Chavez of Chimayo, New Mexico, says. "It's a sure thing. No upkeep, no repair, no problems with cylinders or switches. That's how I did my truck."

Although lowering a vehicle is an important

first step, owners often choose to paint their vehicles first because other changes are expensive and may have to be delayed until owners can come up with the money or enlist someone to help. Candy colors are popular with lowriders—bright apple-red, lemon-drop yellow, lime green, or a special chameleon-change-before-your-eyes color combination head up the list of choices. Much to the delight of lowriders, paints have improved over the years. "We used to have to use enamel paints that ran too easily," Dennis Chavez says. "Now the kids have acrylic paints that are much easier to handle. It works well to put on several coats of acrylic, even layering different colors for special effects. Then most of

Chris Martinez installs a hydraulic system on his lowrider. Using hydraulics, owners can lower and raise their vehicles with the flick of a switch. Hydraulics also give a vehicle its juice to jump, buck, and hop.

Frank Chavez's Chevy Impala boasts a beautiful chrome job on its rear exterior. Customizing a vehicle with surface chrome is a quick and sure way to draw attention, but many owners also chrome their hidden engines and undercarriages simply because they like to.

them put on many coats of clear paint to give a shiny finish."

For a quick and dazzling effect, chrome is a popular addition to lowriders. Chrome wheel rims are almost a "must" for a lowrider—highlighting the small wheels and showing off brightly as the vehicles slowly cruise the roads or parks on a Sunday afternoon. Looking at the outside of a lowrider is often only half of what a viewer sees. Chrome on undercarriages and engine parts makes an impressive display as well. Some owners manage to dress up every part of the engine under the hood with gold or silver plate. Most who have gone to that much trouble to brighten up their vehicles drive them only when necessary. Keeping dirt, oil, grime, and engine wear to a minimum means less maintenance and keeps the car shiny and clean.

Chrome, along with attention-getting paint, is a first choice for customizing a lowrider bicycle. Handlebars, mirrors, rims, and seats dazzle with sparkling chrome for a prize-wining look. Why do people spend so much money on a bicycle? Lilian Robles of the Raza Unida Club in Tucson, Arizona, has an answer. "A lowrider is more than a bike. It's a culture. It is pride which comes from the heart, an important part of our Chicano [Mexican-American] community."

For many lowriders, chrome, paint, and hydraulics are not enough to satisfy their creative urges. Some owners reshape parts of their vehicles' bodies until the original look has completely vanished. Owners say that the older cars that are made of soft, pliable metals can be bent and curved and coaxed into most any shape.

Some lowriders choose "frenching" to modify the look of the body. Owners remove parts of the vehicle below the body, smoothing over the area and creating a new, depressed spot. Then they install headlights or taillights, an antenna or door handles, or even a bumper. Nothing protrudes above the surface, and the vehicle is sleek and new, looking nothing like the original.

A vehicle's profile can also be changed by channeling or chopping the body. Channeling is sawing through the middle and lower parts of a car, removing two or three inches from the vehicle's height. Chopping is taking height off the top of the vehicle, reducing the size of the windshield and windows as well. Both channeling and chopping require special skill because of the risk of ruining the vehicle when cutting through windows, door frames, and roof beams.

Yet another option are suicide openings, in which the doors, trunks, or hoods of the vehicles open in the opposite direction from their original construction. For example, the hoods are modified so that they open from the side, the trunks lift from behind the back window or from the side, and the door openings are closest to the front of the vehicle. With these and other modifications, lowriders maintain their reputation. They take what exists and creatively and deliberately make it work another way.

The earliest lowriders were plainer than today's high-tech cars and trucks. At one time, a slick paint job and fine customization were enough to make the owners' desired statements, but not now. Today's prize-winning lowriders have become rolling galleries for artists who use every inch of space available to display their talents. Inside door jambs, under fenders, the back sides of mirrors, or the engine blocks are transformed to add details much like the tattoos on human skin.

Long before their work is completed, owners must decide who or what their wheels will represent. Do I want to honor Mexican history so that onlookers will get the message? Does my lowrider honor some family tradition? Will it be a reflection of me, the owner, only? "My car is me," John Moore of Kansas City says. "I am plain. I am straight. I am uncomplicated and what you see is what you get. That describes my old '86 Chevy that I bought to drive around and have fun. I don't make it fancy because I'm not fancy. I don't want to have to protect delicate paint jobs or expensive

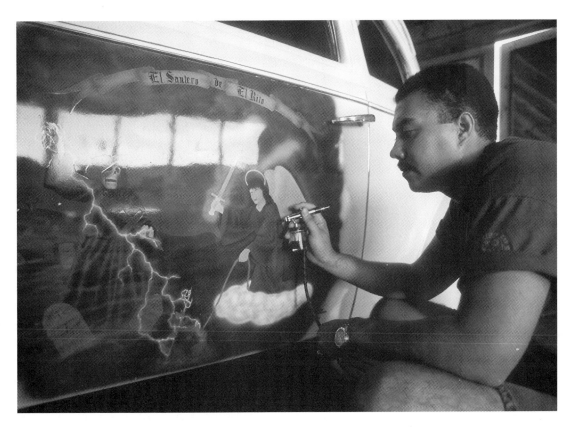

chrome. My car reminds me of who I am. I may change the car, but it will be because I changed something about me first."

Those who have specific ideas about what their cars are to represent use murals, large paintings, to carry their messages. For example, Mexican history is very important to David Leon of Wichita, Kansas, founder of the Reflections Car Club. His cars speak about his allegiance to the Aztec Native Americans who resisted the Spanish invasion of Mexico in the 16th century. Leon includes the word "Atzlan" (the Aztecs' name for themselves) in the names of his cars and paints the Aztec god Huitzilpochtli in the murals on each of his vehicles.

Desi Lopez, an artist who decorates many lowriders, applies his talents to a car door. Images and murals on lowriders are important expressions of their owners' ideas and beliefs.

Not only must a lowrider reflect a certain image, it must also express a certain sound. Top quality sound systems make lowriders really cool. The louder the music, the better, but the sound has to be balanced with woofers and tweeters carefully chosen and placed in the vehicle to show off the owner's favorite music.

Making plans for, and creating, a lowrider are as varied as the owner's concept of his ultimate vehicle. Shoppers see piles of metal scraps that used to be an old Chevy or a Ford and draw pictures in their minds of what could be. Beginning with an old heap often costs the least money to get started. "I got my Chevy for $400," John Moore says. "It was in pretty bad shape. For another $200, I got new doors and fenders. A friend sold me hydraulics for $700. Another friend did the body work for $200, so until I replace the hydraulics with better ones, I have a fun runnin' car for not too much money."

Jae Brattain of the Uso Car Clubs in California points out that different sections of the United States have their own styles of lowriders. "We in Southern California are trendsetters," he explains. "We are innovators with big imaginations. Others copy us in a few years. Right now we're doing far-out murals— medieval fantasy patterns, mermaids and pirates . . . We have many great artists here. . . . Our level of craftsmanship is very high and always evolving. We show others how to do it."

If owners don't like their first modifications or if they can't even decide which modifications to make first, they need only notice other lowriders. To keep people looking at cars and to keep winning prizes, owners must make regular changes anyway, hopefully more beautiful, more sleek, more unique each time. Lowriders need not be concerned about making perfect customizing decisions. What is most important is that the dream and the love are expressed no matter how owners choose to fashion their vehicles. As Christina Casado, wife of Mariano Casado of the Oldies Car Club of East Bay, California, says, "You can count on us to be the same as we've always been—loyal to our friends and focused on our families. We show that love with our old cars too."

THE LOWRIDER HERITAGE

There are several stories about the origins of modern-day lowriders. One tells about the Moors, a Muslim people who invaded Spain in the 700s, whose horses and riders were decked out in fancy decorations. Some think the Spaniards adopted the Moorish idea of dressing up their horses and took it with them to the New World when they invaded Mexico in the 1500s. From this came the tradition of creating fancy contemporary vehicles.

Another story involves modern-day Chicanos. Chicanos, the story goes, did not like the plain look-alike cars produced in the United States after World War II. While middle-class non-Hispanic families flocked to Chevrolet or Ford dealers for a new car, Mexican Americans found a way to make a statement by distinctively fixing up their older cars. They would have no look-alikes, nothing commonplace. This drew attention to them as a special group of people and helped them feel closer to their original roots and more united in a common cause. Whether

David Lopez poses with his 1963 Chevy Impala Super Sport outside a church in Sorroco, New Mexico. For Hispanic lowriders, their vehicles become a symbol of their roots and traditions and help them keep their heritage alive.

Mexican Americans or Hispanics from other Spanish-speaking nations, they began to be recognized as Americans with their own ideas.

Whatever the origins of the lowriders, they made their presence fully known in Southern California beginning in the 1940s with the *pauchuco* movement. (*Pauchuco* is Spanish for the best lowrider.) That decade was a time of unrest for Mexican Americans, many of whom were discriminated against and often mistreated. Conflicts with Anglos (non-Hispanic citizens) led to riots in Los Angeles.

In spite of the turmoil, Mexican Americans found ways to define themselves as a special people. After all, they thought, other people who live in the United States have also come from somewhere else, and we Mexican Americans will make a statement about ourselves just as they have.

Adopting zoot suits (a distinctive outfit), ducktail hair styles, and a swaggering walk, Mexican Americans began to distinguish themselves as a people who are colorful, proud, and strong. Most of all, they chose a type of vehicle to represent them—the lowrider. Other groups had hot rods and drag-racing cars with elevated front ends and big tires for fast racing. The new lowrider would attract attention by being just the opposite. It would have elevated back ends, smaller tires, and move slowly.

No one knows for sure what event might have been "the" moment when lowriders began, but lowrider owners like to talk about the possibilities. They often identify themselves with an idea and keep it alive by telling how they or their clubs or families do lowriding.

One tradition that lowriders may reflect is that

of the Spanish style, borrowed from the Moors, of decorating horses and riders. It is possible that the impression the Spaniards made on the Native Americans when they invaded Mexico was so strong that the memories lasted for centuries, long enough to influence the design of lowriders.

The Spanish conquest brought more than a style of decoration, however. With the Spaniards came a different religion, language, and tradition. Over the years the new ways combined with the old to create a mixture of Spaniards and Native Americans and a new Mexican culture. Aztecs and other Native American groups adopted Roman Catholicism, the religion of the Spaniards. Along with new rituals, the Mexican people began

Arthur "Lolo" Medina of Chimayo, New Mexico, has chosen to adorn his 1976 Cadillac with religious images and has named his vehicle "Lowrider Heaven." Like Arthur, many other lowriders express their faith through the religious icons they display on their vehicles.

to revere the icons of Christianity—saints, the Holy Family, the Resurrected Jesus, and the Virgin Mary.

As the Spanish expanded their conquest northward from Mexico, many Mexicans moved into what is now the Southwest of the United States. Generations later, when Mexican Americans began decorating their lowriders, they incorporated the Christian icons. Today's lowriders often paint images of Jesus, the Holy Family, and the Virgin Mary on doors, hoods, and trunks of vehicles to honor a religion adopted so long ago.

While Aztecs in Mexico adopted Roman Catholicism, they did not entirely forget the old ways. As time passed, they often combined Aztec rituals and traditions into the new religion—and still do. To honor their distant Aztec ancestors and their ancient traditions, some lowriders display Aztec icons on their vehicles. One might see colorful images of Tloque Nahuaque, the warrior god, or Montezuma II, the last of the Aztec emperors.

Although so many contemporary lowriders are beautifully decorated, the first vehicles were clean and plain. By the 1960s, though, owners were creating vehicles as works of art. "Gypsy Rose," a lowrider owned by Jesse Valdez, led the way. Jesse's 1964 Chevy Impala was covered with 150 pink, red, and white roses, totaling more than 2,500 painted petals. Shaved door handles and emblems, a donut steering wheel, and hydraulics to lay the car down for a cool look and lift it back up for a good ride helped "Gypsy Rose" become a world-famous lowrider.

When production of the television show *Chico and the Man* began in 1974, the NBC network

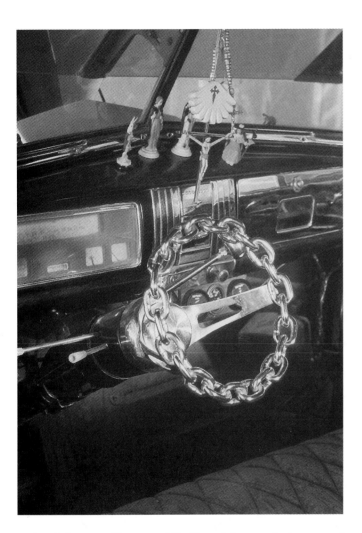

A chain-link steering wheel and religious icons are part of the interior decoration of Nicholas Herrera's 1939 Chevy Coupe. As well as the outside appearance, owners take pride in the interiors of their lowriders, often devoting a great deal of time and money to capture the right effect.

asked Jesse if he would allow his car to be used for opening shots on the show. Jesse said yes. "Gypsy Rose" quickly became the best-known lowrider in the world, and soon viewers who saw the lowrider every week on TV started asking questions. What is this car? Who knows how to make one? How do I get one?

The opportunities to design and show off lowriders expanded as hydraulics were introduced. A lowrider with hydraulics cruising the

When Jerome Reynolds of Alcalde, New Mexico, wanted to express his beliefs, he imagined the image of Jesus on his 1950 Chevy Fleetline and asked artist Randy Martinez to make his vision reality.

streets was a spectacle waiting to happen. The flick of a switch turned a slow rider into a kicking mule, one wheel at a time.

Ruben Gonzalez knows about the spectacle hydraulics can create. He transformed a well-worn pickup inherited from his father into a hard-hitting, mad-hopping dance machine with a 12-battery hydraulic setup. Those who watched the reborn truck jump, jerk, and jolt named it the "Wicked One."

Hydraulics was only the first of numerous modifications made to the "Wicked One," all of which eventually cost Ruben about $50,000. The vehicle sports a chopped top, a channeled frame, and a custom see-through bed. Purple velvet upholstery shows off hundreds of hand-cut mirrors placed throughout, and the entire undercarriage is chrome-plated or painted with candy-blue and purple flakes. Custom air-brushed murals of dragons and wizards on the doorjambs, hood, dash, and tailgate guarantee attention wherever Ruben drives. The "Wicked One" is one of the most famous lowriders today.

By the 1970s, lowriders had gone public. In New Mexico, the towns of Chimayo and Española became the self-declared lowrider capitals of the world. Mexican Americans in the towns turned into engineers and, with their families, converted weathered heaps of metal into elegant works of art. What was once a mass-produced '50s Chevy became a reminder of a decorated horse and rider. Large religious murals on hoods and doors, small carved wooden saints on the dash, or rosaries circling the mirrors kept the lowriders of New Mexico close to their roots.

Another major encouragement for lowriders in the 1970s was the advent of *Lowrider* magazine, started by Sonny Madrid and a few other loyal founders. As a student at San Jose State University in California, Sonny became involved in publications that promote stories and events with a Chicano theme. Early efforts to fund his ideas were difficult, but Sonny had a core belief about what needed to happen for his people and for the idea of lowriders.

Sonny and his team worked hard, recruiting support door-to-door and building up a group of dedicated followers and contributors. By January 1977, 1,000 copies of the first issue of *Lowrider* had been hand-delivered throughout northern California, an event that began a continuing mission to present the lowriding lifestyle to the nation and the world.

Overcoming prejudice and discrimination against Mexican Americans and facing a public that thought lowriders meant violence took time. By 1979, Sonny and his friends managed to schedule a lowrider show at the Gila River Indian Reservation south of Phoenix, Arizona. Off-limits to city and state authorities, the location provided the place where a successful, peaceful event occurred. Police, who had announced that the show would be a gang event, could only stand and watch.

Word spread that lowrider shows were exciting entertainment, not promotions of violence and crime, and by the 1980s, Sonny and his group were holding them all across the country. Successful national lowrider shows also boosted the popularity of *Lowrider* magazine, not only spreading the positive influence of lowriders but giving the magazine photos and stories for every issue.

Lowrider magazine sponsors tours at which winning for the best vehicle has become important for lowriders who want recognition and prizes. Winners become eligible to compete in a national supershow at the close of a year's tour. Not only do owners receive publicity, they can also win prize money, in some shows as much as $2,500. Better yet, car shows encourage positive publicity for the entire lowrider lifestyle.

By the 1990s, lowriders had become integrated into the car culture of the United States, with credit for the movement's origin going to Mexican Americans. Some of the bad rap still remained, however. Some perceive lowriders as people with big cars and no jobs, implying that these fancy vehicles are paid for by theft or drug money. Despite such ideas, most of those in the movement focus on the positive side of lowriding.

People of different ages, economic levels, and ethnic backgrounds are represented in car clubs everywhere. Lowriding has become an accepted way to have fun, be responsible, and stay out of trouble. "When something has made a big enough impression, others want to copy it," explains Lonnie Lopez, editor and creative director of *Lowrider* magazine. "That is what's happened with lowriders and I think it's a very good thing."

GIVING MEANING TO LOWRIDERS

From the beginning of the movement, lowriders have always stood for something. It may be obvious or it may be hidden, even mysterious and unknown at first. Eventually, though, lowriders became a representation of their owners. An owner almost never creates a lowrider without a specific purpose. To discover a lowrider's meaning, ask the owner. Usually the more meaning owners place on their vehicles, the more confident and assured they feel about themselves.

For some, lowriders symbolize memories. Raul Tostado's car is about his past. When Raul was two years old, his father was killed in the Vietnam war. For some 20 years, Raul's mother kept alive for him the image of his father as a loving, giving man. When Raul turned 18, he received money his father had left for him to use as he pleased.

The young man decided he wanted a car, and

Each lowrider attaches meaning to a vehicle, something that represents himself or a purpose. For Floyd Montoya of Córdova, New Mexico, restoring a 1952 Chevy Fleetline helped him overcome some hard times. Over the years, creating lowriders has given Floyd a tremendous sense of accomplishment. "It keeps me going in the right direction," he says.

35

Lowriders remember not only their history or traditions through their vehicles but also departed loved ones. Keeping alive precious moments inspired Atanacio "Tiny" Romero of Chimayo to dedicate his 1975 Chevy Caprice to the memory of Lucia, a deceased family member.

he bought a 1995 Toyota Camry. As Raul thought about how he wanted his car to look and the meaning he wanted to project, he told his mother what he had in mind—a memorial to his father. Although pleased, she said she would not believe it until she saw it.

In his mind's eye, Raul pictured a painting honoring his father which would represent both the past and the present. As the image took shape, he imagined his father in his Marine uniform with scenes of the war in the background. As Raul described his idea to a painter, hoping the concept would work, the artist proposed a mural centering around the image of Raul's father in heaven with Jesus and surrounded by clouds and war scenes in the background.

As Raul relates, "I told the painter I wanted a scene so when someone comes by, they'll notice. I liked the painter's ideas. He did a great job. But as it turned out, the part I liked best was the paint job on the rest of the car. It's chameleon. When you look at it from the front, you see green. From the back it seems purple, and looking at it straight on from the side it looks yellow. I decided the color changes represent Vietnam flashbacks. If Dad had lived through the war, he would probably be having flashbacks like other soldiers do now. It's really cool."

Raul named his car "Memories of War." The symbol of his father's life and what he gave Raul in spite of his death mean the most to Raul. He will never give up his car. "I'll keep working on it," he says, "like putting chrome on the undercarriage this winter. I take it to car shows because I like to be looked at like other lowriders do. But I have deeper reasons. The car honors Dad. I want it to represent the war for all who were in Vietnam. When veterans come by, they ask me about it and then I can tell my story again."

Like Raul's painter who pictured an image of Jesus, many other lowriders choose religious icons in their vehicles' murals. To Mexican Americans, depictions of the Virgin of Guadalupe are especially significant, for she is the patron saint of Mexico.

According to tradition, after the Spanish conquest, a young Aztec boy named Juan Diego who had converted to Christianity experienced a vision. On a hill called Tepeyac outside Mexico City, the Virgin Mary appeared to Juan, directing him to tell the Catholic bishop to build a church in her honor so that she could give love, hope, and protection to all Mexican people.

When the bishop demanded proof of Juan's vision, the boy returned to Tepeyac hill, where the Virgin appeared again and gave Juan a sign— clusters of fragrant red roses suddenly bloomed on the hill even though it was December. As the Virgin guided him, Juan gathered the flowers and folded them into his cloak to present them to the bishop.

When Juan unwrapped his cloak for the bishop, flowers tumbled at his feet and an image appeared on the boy's cloak. It was the face of the Virgin Mary, permanently imprinted on the cloak. Convinced that Juan was indeed delivering a holy message, the leaders of the Catholic Church built a magnificent cathedral. The image from Juan's cloak, known as the Miraculous Portrait, hangs in the cathedral of Our Lady of Guadalupe in Mexico City, the great church built to honor the Virgin Mary.

Mexicans and Mexican Americans always celebrate December 12, the day that the Virgin of Guadalupe revealed herself to Juan. To honor the miracle of the roses given to Juan, people lay masses of the brightly colored flowers on private and public shrines to remember the Virgin's appearance. She has come to stand for hope, charity, loyalty, protection, and unfailing loving kindness. Followers trust her to help, cure, and protect them, just as she promised she would.

One such follower is Jose Valarde. His '84 Chevy Camaro often joins other lowriders that fill the parking lot of the Santuario de Chimayo, an old Catholic church in the town of Chimayo, where miracles are said to have occurred. Most of the vehicles display devotional images. One shows a panoramic view of the town, including

the church itself. Another depicts the Resurrection and Ascension of Jesus in bright blue and green. All are beautiful displays, but one car truly stands out. On Jose's car, the Virgin of Guadalupe stands tall on the hood.

Presenting lowriders' religious icons to the world is the work of artists such as Randy Martinez of Chimayo, who is considered a master at turning cars like that of Jose Valarde into a religious statement. Through the art of Randy and others, vehicles become icons of faith, truly rolling chapels, proving that lowriders are a unique way to honor, display, and communicate what their owners honor and believe.

Many lowrider owners are especially fond of

Remembering the story of the Virgin of Guadalupe and the miracle of the roses, Eddie Gallegos of El Llano symbolized his religious roots through the mural of the Virgin Mary on his 1964 Chevy Impala.

floral decorations, and traditions abound about how roses have come to be meaningful symbols in decorating vehicles. One is the story of the roses of the Virgin of Guadalupe. Another tells that as Jesus prayed before his death, the tears he shed miraculously became red roses as they dropped to the ground. Roses on lowriders serve to remind believers of Jesus' pain and their belief in his gift of salvation.

Other rose images may symbolize the tradition of Moorish decorations. The Moors often encircled the necks of their horses with garlands of roses. When modern-day lowriders solder gold- or chrome-plated chain links together to make steering wheels, they are reflecting Moorish designs. Shown against the purple, red, or green velvet upholstery, the effect is dazzling.

Many owners pay tribute to their heroes through their lowriders. As you have read, many honor their Aztec heritage through depictions of warrior gods or great leaders. Others honor more current figures whom they admire and respect. Victor Garcia's "Purple Haze" Mazda truck memorializes Jimi Hendrix, a famous rock guitarist from the 1960s. "I'm a pace setter in using this kind of symbol," Victor says. "It gets attention and that's good. I can tell the story of Jimi with murals, quotes, and pictures of him performing. I change the murals nearly every year to make it interesting for me and for those who see my truck often."

Victor is pleased to honor Hendrix's life and music and through his truck remembers that Jimi was popular in England around the same time the Beatles came to the United States. The Hendrix family planned a celebration in the fall of 2000 to commemorate Jimi's life, and they invited Victor and his truck to join them in England for the festivities.

Lowrider Arthur Medina of Chimayo remembers his hero, Elvis Presley, with the colorful murals on his 1967 Pontiac. Arthur feels that Elvis was influenced by the *pauchuco* movement in the 1940s and showed the look with the duck-tail hair style, the swagger walk, and a breathy singing style.

For Dave Jaramillo, there was the dream. He wanted a lowrider so clean and mean, so low and slow that it would win in the biggest lowrider shows. Dave died in a tragic accident before he could make the dream come true, and his family completed the planned changes. From 1979 to 1982, his lowrider, "Dave's Dream," won numerous events, including the Best Lowrider award, throughout New Mexico.

Dave's family stored and cared for the car until 1990, when, through the efforts of Dr. Benito Cordova, the Smithsonian Institution in Washington, D.C., bought the lowrider. "Technically, 'Dave's Dream' may be a '69 Ford LTD, but that's the least important fact about the car," Dr. Cordova has explained. "The whole point of building a lowrider is to erase the manufacturer's imprint and then make a reflection of the owner's soul. Every lowrider is after a dream, as was Dave."

Dr. Cordova believes that "Dave's Dream" is the first lowrider to become part of a permanent museum collection. Most lowriders remain in a state of transition, being repainted, shortened or lengthened, chromed or frenched, each time their owners are struck by a new idea. But as Dr. Cordova put it, "Dave's Dream" may be one of the only lowriders ever to be finally "finished."

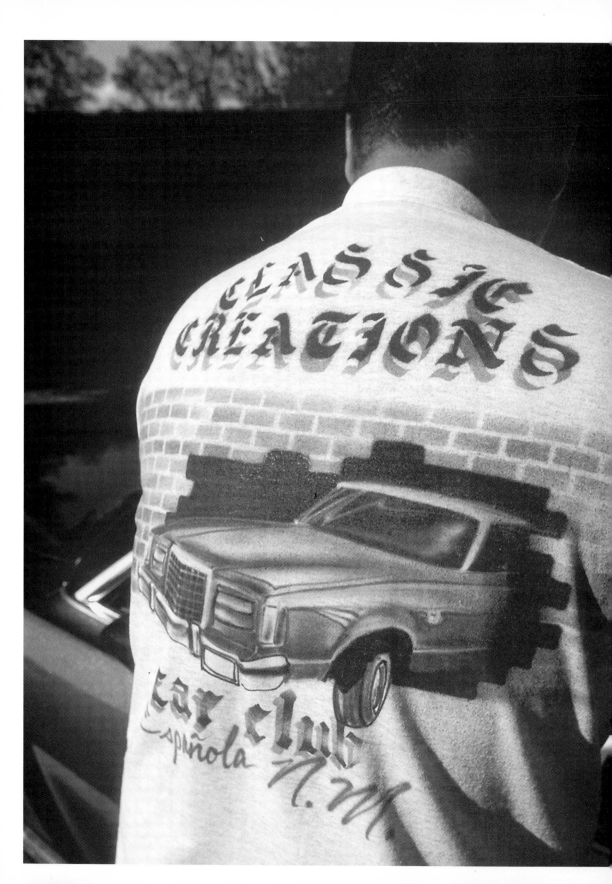

GETTING TOGETHER
IN CAR CLUBS

For lowriders, car clubs offer a way to enjoy the company of their fellow owners, talk about their vehicles, show them off, and learn from one another. Some clubs focus mainly on the vehicles; others emphasize how members use their time and conduct their lives. Some do not even require members to own cars or have intentions of acquiring them. With new car clubs popping up somewhere every day, lowriders and potential lowriders have no problem finding a club to suit their needs.

Chicano Playaz, a club founded by Victor Garcia, admits only lowrider cars and trucks. No other vehicles are allowed. The club votes on the vehicles as well as on owners to see if they are qualified for membership. "We take in winners," says Victor, "no dents, no rust, it must be nice. For example, if we take 18 entries to a car show, we usually come home

Lee Cordova sports a shirt displaying the logo of his car club in Española, New Mexico. Lowrider car clubs, which have been formed across the country, are an important part of lowriding. Not only do they offer members a sense of unity, most also support community activities and help promote lowriding as a responsible and honorable part of America's car culture.

with 17 winners. We want the recognition. We want to overcome [the] bad rap for lowriders. We're known as the picky club."

These are serious lowriders. To be a fully recognized member of the Chicano Playaz Club, members must have made four major modifications to their cars or trucks. Members must also have installed hydraulics or intend to do so. Tinted windows, customized paint, stereo systems, and interior all count. Adding murals anywhere on the vehicle also counts.

Chicano Playaz is a nonprofit organization with 23 chapters in Texas, Oklahoma, Arkansas, Indiana, Illinois, Minnesota, and Kansas that work hard to maintain standards. "We have a good name," Victor explains. "No drugs, no gangs. We host car shows and we judge car shows. Others who want to put on successful car shows pay us to use our name. With the money we make, we give to charity functions and sponsor school projects." He adds, "We have very strict rules."

The purpose of the River City Rod and Custom Car Club of Wichita, Kansas, is quite different from that of Chicano Playaz. Members own older cars, some customized as lowriders, some restored to their original condition, and some still quite plain. Once a month during spring and summer, owners and their families receive a newsletter announcing when and where to meet for a 40 to 60 mile Sunday Fun Day Cruise.

All together, the lowriders cruise slowly along the road, feeling free and enjoying the glances from onlookers. Reaching their destination, members park their vehicles (sometimes as many as 50) as close together as possible. It's a

leisurely get-together as they relax, talk about their lowriders, and return home in a slowly moving caravan.

Doug Strahan, a member of River City Rod and Custom says that "We old guys like to go back to the days of big cars. You can get your car, your look with an old car. When I was a boy growing up in the 1960s, I couldn't afford a nice car. Now I can, so I find big cars like Cadillacs that I wanted as a teenager and restore them to their original condition. There's no better way for me to relax than to work on my car, get together with club members, and cruise down the road. I pull up memories of my

David Lopez proudly announces the name of his car club, Touch of Class, on his Chevy Impala. Following a positive lifestyle and maintaining a top-quality vehicle are mandatory in most car clubs.

younger years and change them to go the way I wanted."

February 1995 marked the beginning of the Reflections Car Club, which now has 11 chapters in 9 states. The membership is a reflection of American society, including all different groups, political views, and religions. And the club's major purpose is aiding a variety of social, educational, and civic causes. "We interview groups and individuals before making decisions about who gets our money," says David Leon, a founder of the club. "We give scholarships and help with other multi-racial activities such as literacy campaigns, voter registration groups, and children's advocacy groups. We started the club with some broad plans, but soon decided we wanted a specific, really high level purpose."

Membership in Reflections means taking full responsibility for a positive lifestyle as a lowrider in a multicultural society. Members express themselves through their vehicles and agree to maintain a top-quality show car at all times. They must show that they lead by example by how they present their lowriders and how they drive them in public. Membership in Reflections is an individual effort, and it is serious.

The car club Raza Unida ("United Race") patterns itself after a community program in Santa Cruz, California, called Barrios Unidos. Both the club and Barrios Unidos ("Communities United") focus on violence prevention among youth by offering positive alternatives. Daniel Alejandrez (Nane, as he is known), founder of Barrios Unidos, and Vincente Lujano, founder of Raza Unida, believe strongly that lowriders are an excellent option for young people. Nane describes how the club reaches out to the community:

> We use lowriders in our outreach program several ways. We get car clubs together for celebrations such as *Cinco de Mayo* [the Fifth of May, a special Mexican holiday] and the Fourth of July to show how lowriders are a good way to spend time and energy. When we do our work in prisons, lowriders are a great topic for conversation. Inmates get out of their mental prison environment for a few moments by looking at lowriders and talking about them. They may remember someone they knew who had a lowrider or they may want to own one when they get out of prison. Many are sophisticated enough to know about paint jobs and tires and the mechanics of our lowriders. We talk to them about the art of lowriding. We bring a little bit of the outside world to their inside world.

Vincente Lujano is involved in drug-prevention programs as well as programs to keep young people out of gangs. Targeting kids in middle and high schools, he explains alternative activities, including being lowriders. Vincente speaks to the young people from his own experience; he owns a lowrider, a 1979 Monte Carlo that wins prizes. "It's a good model for them—custom paint job, upholstery, hydraulics, and sound system," he says. "Just like a typical lowrider, I'm starting to redo the car again. They learn from me about always wanting to improve."

Twenty-five years after its founding in 1975, Three Individuals Car Club is one of the most famous in the United States. Once a club of 26 members but now having only four, Three Individuals is still as strong as ever, having held its best, if not biggest, annual Fresno Super Car Show in 1999.

Of the four members, three are named Martinez. Pete and Louie are brothers; Don Martinez is a longtime family friend. The fourth member is another longtime friend, Paul Avila. By now the club is more like family than a just a quartet of members. The four work hard to maintain the quality and integrity of the club name, which long ago was trademarked and patented for their use only.

Pete Martinez, the club's president, is proud of their history and their dedication to mounting quality shows for every member of a family, no matter what the family members' ages are. As Pete describes it, "Young ones bring their bicycles and model cars to show. They are learning about paints and patience and keeping their wheels clean. It's a great lesson in responsibility. They're starting a hobby that keeps them involved in positive things."

Three Individuals' objective is to banish entirely the negative stereotype of the lowrider. Where once lowriders were looked upon as people with fancy cars but no jobs, now they are seen as supporters of the community, members of close-knit families, and talented artists. As much as any community group, Three Individuals Car Club has given lowriders a positive image. "Anywhere we go, people know us," Pete says. "We are proud of our track record."

How does it feel to be the largest lowrider club in the world? "That's not our goal," answers Jae Brattain, the Uso Club's chief executive officer. "We like to win, but that's not our goal either."

Lowriders Ray Ortiz and his son, Ray Jr., pose with their 1958 Chevy Impala outside their art gallery in Chimayo.

The car club Uso takes its name from the word that means "brothers"—very close brothers—in the language of the Samoan people. Samoa is a nation of nine islands in the South Pacific Ocean. Kita Lealao and some close friends from Samoa started the club in October 1992 in the harbor area of Los Angeles, California. The group chose tough guidelines. It would be family oriented, but more importantly, no color barriers would exist. The club's major goal is to foster close-knit groups of "brothers" throughout the club network, just as the name says.

In 1998, when *Lowrider* magazine named Uso the Car Club of the Year, owners who read about the award realized that Uso had chapters in places other than California. Ten more

Thanks to the efforts of car clubs and lowrider publications, supershows can bring trophies, honors, and prize money for club members. Geraldine Gallegos garnered a blanketful of awards at a 1993 show in Las Vegas, Nevada.

chapters popped up in a flash, as 22 chapters expanded to 32. From Miami to San Diego, from Seattle to New York, more than 300 Uso members abide by a set of 43 rules and regulations.

Members must behave honorably and act as brothers who support and care about one another. The cars must be just as impressive as well: knock-off wire wheels only, clean at all times, and new improvements on the vehicles every three months. To reinforce the idea of owner and wheels as one, members must drive their lowriders to every club meeting, unless the vehicle is under construction. "We insist on cleanliness in our cars and in our lives," Jae says. "We also emphasize attention to detail, high level customization that's up to our standards. Nothing less."

For those who want to find a car club to join, members of the clubs described above advise carefully checking out each club. Most clubs and members are responsible and work toward honorable goals. Some clubs, however, do use lowriders as a cover for drug activity or forming gangs. Would-be lowriders can judge such clubs, which are called "thugs" by legitimate clubs, by finding out how members behave and watching their actions. Thug meetings plan drug drops and trades, and their vehicles carry out the plans. Money to customize thug lowriders can come from illegal activities.

Ask questions, listen to the answers, and watch carefully to make good choices. Obtain statements of a club's goals, investigate how it uses its money, and find out how a club involves itself in the community. The truest of lowriders make owning a beautiful vehicle an honorable, cooperative way to build family togetherness and encourage strong friendships.

SOME LOWRIDERS AND THEIR SCENES

Like the fast-growing Mexican-American population, the lowrider movement is expanding too. Chicanos, however, are not the only group of Americans who are part of the lowrider phenomenon. Anyone who likes to work on cars and create a different and exciting vehicle can be a lowrider and enjoy the thrill of lowriding.

Dennis Chavez of the Chimayo, New Mexico, Valley Cruisers Car Club greatly enjoys the scene at his club. In addition to earning money that has supported projects such as the kindergarten and Head Start programs, Dennis and his fellow lowriders show off their vehicles whenever possible. As he has explained, "We would cruise to Taos or Santa Fe on the weekends. We would go regular speed up there, always staying together in the right lane. When we got to Taos, we set up a nice cruise on the Main Plaza. People came out to see our cars."

Dennis purchased his Ford truck, "Blue Angel," from his father-in-law in 1973 and slowly began to

From its origins among Mexican Americans, lowriding has opened up to include people of all ages and ethnic backgrounds. Anyone who loves to customize and maintain a vehicle and dress it up as elegantly as this pickup can be part of the lowrider movement.

customize it. First, he attached new rims and pipes and gave the Ford a paint job. His velvet upholstery was done by his wife; bucket seats, a console with television, and sunroof were last. "It was a prize winner," Dennis declares proudly. But he does remind people that lowriders are never quite finished. Dennis has painted his truck four times and plans to keep it in tip-top shape for his grandson. In the meantime, he cruises in the summer and stores his truck from October to April.

A favorite moment for Dennis as a lowrider was a visit to the *Good Morning America* show with then host David Hartman. The Chimayo Chamber of Commerce recommended Dennis for an interview, and Hartman invited Dennis to the show. Dennis videotaped one of his cruises, and it aired on the show. "I had people call and tell me they liked the video and they liked what I had to say," he recalls. "I just tell lowriders to stay on the right. Take your time. Don't block both lanes. It gets you in trouble with the police. Besides, people can't see you and then you've missed the point."

It was 1980 and Jack Salezar knew about problems brewing between the Austin, Texas, police and Austin lowriders. Thinking that holding a car show might be a good idea, Jack checked out the rules and regulations that would apply to a lowrider show. Working with a friend, Red Garcia, Jack set up a car show involving as many car clubs as would participate.

One of the purposes of the car show was to unite car clubs, and the show's success led to the formation of the Austin Lowriders Association. Ten clubs joined—including a Harley motorcycle club—and the association was going strong,

especially in its support of community projects. As Jack explains, "We bought a van for battered women. We sent kids to summer camp. We got a lot of good publicity."

The Austin Lowriders Association was active until 1984 when interest in lowriders in Austin fizzled, mostly because car shows became less popular. But with new interest in lowriders brewing in the 1990s, Jack was approached to recharge the association. "I was still cruising," Jack says, "and the young guys respected me for that. The Association has more than a dozen clubs now."

The organization holds picnics and other events for all the families and works closely

An elaborate, eye-catching child's bike is on display at a lowrider show. Lowriders, whether young or old, are not restricted to any one kind of vehicle. They have the freedom to choose whatever pleases them and expresses their feelings.

Lowrider Annette Gonzales likes to cruise behind the wheel of her customized 1978 Chevy Monte Carlo. Annette and many other women are showing off their skills and talent in what was once only a man's activity.

with the Austin Police Department in sponsoring events such as the campaign to gather toys for children.

Jack also gives lowrider presentations at schools in the area and has received a grant to set up workshops about building lowriders. He can talk authentically about the subject because of his 1950 Pontiac Chieftain. "It's all original," Jack says. "Hub caps, wheels, gray interior, everything. But I do have hydraulics on it and of course that is not original."

As a college student in Houston, Texas, Francisco Pena needed a topic for a speech-class assignment. "I wanted to do something different and I had just gotten into lowriding. So

I had this idea about hydraulics. Have my car club friends bring their lowriders, demonstrate, and then talk about how you do hydraulics. My teacher thought it was a good idea."

On the day of the presentation, Francisco and his friends blocked off a section of the parking lot, set up a table with lowrider literature, including a hydraulic kit with cylinders, pumps, and motors. When the time came for the one-minute "show," a friend turned on loud music, and for a full minute, two demonstration lowriders bucked, bounced, jumped, and hopped. Students clapped, screamed, and danced, and others poured out of classes to check out the commotion. By the time Francisco got to the information part of the speech, he had a huge audience.

Francisco spoke about Raul Aguirre, the Los Angeles lowrider credited with developing the first hydraulic system on a car. Raul had a problem. He had lowered his '54 Chevy Corvette by cutting the springs on the vehicle, and the job was permanent. Because the police had laws about how many inches cars must be from the ground, Raul kept getting tickets. He wondered why he couldn't find a way to put his car up or down when he wanted to.

Raul's search for a solution led him to the airplane junkyards, where he found hydraulic systems from discarded airplane landing gear. Describing the process, Francisco explained to the students that "getting the parts was one tough thing. But installing them was even tougher." He went on to tell how Raul found a way to raise his car while driving and lower it when he parked. The Chevy didn't hop and dance as lowriders do now, but installing the

For many lowriders, the most important part of their lifestyle is passing on the tradition from father to son. Young B. J. Vigil of Española, posing with his father, Benny, is already learning the lowrider tradition and culture with his own minivehicle.

hydraulics took care of Raul's problem with the police.

The rest of Francisco's speech concerned cylinders, pumps, and hoses. When he concluded his presentation, his audience asked numerous questions of him and his friends and then wanted to get into the demonstration cars to experience the feel of a lowrider.

Francisco's speech was a hit, and he got an A for his efforts.

Steve Miller's first car was a 1969 Volkswagen Beetle, which he lowered and fancied up with interior black leather. Steve painted the exterior a burgundy color and chromed the wheels and engine parts. "It was beautiful," he says, "but I got it mostly to have fun. Then I sold it and decided to get serious."

Purchasing a 1995 Honda Civic, he set himself a specific goal: He would see to it that his car, the "Viridian Cruiser," would be featured on the cover of *Lowrider Euro* magazine. Adding air-ride suspension, custom rims, and a slide ragtop, Steve created an interior that was a masterpiece combination of yellow and blue-green to compliment the red exterior.

Steve won trophies at all the shows he entered, and *Lowrider Euro* magazine took notice. The "Viridian Cruiser" was featured in the winter 1999 issue of the magazine. Having reached one goal, what was next for Steve? He would sell the car and get enough money to take on another challenge.

Steve is aware of what is on the market, and he also knows what works well on cars and what does not. As a sales manager for Master Image Customs in Placentia, California, he and his fellow workers have the latest knowledge in modified suspension systems. "I favor air ride suspension systems," Steve says. "Then drivers can make adjustments. Oil suspension systems are not flexible enough for my purpose."

Reanna Garcia of Austin, Texas, is six years old, and already she is winning prizes with her tricycle. Her dad and her uncle built it, and Reanna spends her summers taking the tricycle to shows throughout Texas. "I stand by the trike while we show it," Reanna explains. "I hold a little handle while it sits on a carpet with lights all around. It's painted maroon, and has a beam on the back where others can stand. It has a special circle in the back with a plaque of Jesus. It has a big chrome-plated rim on the front and little rims on the back. It's really fancy."

If she continues her interest in lowriders, Reanna and other kids like her can go on to bigger vehicles because lowriding is here to stay. While lowriding began as a Chicano movement in the 1940s, in the 1990s it hardly showed ethnic, economic, or gender barriers. Lowriders are for anybody who has the desire, imagination, and talent to create one. As a spokeswoman for the Ladies Style Car Club in Oakland, California, said, "Lowriding is a form of showing people who we are. We're just as creative as the dudes can be. We get together and support each other just like they do. Besides, a lowrider driven by a lady always looks better."

Lowriders know what it takes to turn a crumpled-up junker into a shiny, smooth ride that turns heads as it cruises the streets and parks. And they know why they love lowriding. It is about displaying attitudes and beliefs; it is about drama on the street. Lowriders are proud that they transformed a hand-me-down and created a "looker" by being smart and talented.

Victor Lopez of Santa Cruz, California, knows what it means to "just do it." When he redid his '54 Chevy, frenching headlights, door handles, and trunk lid, he knew it was time to redo himself. He sold the car, went to college with the money, and then started over again. Now he has a '49 Chevy that he will channel, chop, french, and finish with a wraparound bumper. "When people turn to look at your car going down the street, it's a real rush and always worth the cost," Victor says.

Solid, stable, and crouched on their haunches hugging the ground, lowriders are ready to spring into action at the flick of a switch. They hop, buck, and kick in healthy rebellion and then settle down to hug the ground again. Those who have a passion for their lowriders have transformed the old tradition of the beautifully decked-out horse and its rider as one into the new idea of lowrider and owner as one.

GLOSSARY

Channeling   Customizing a car or truck by removing a few inches horizontally from the middle of the vehicle. For example, cutting through the doors and fenders.

Chopping   Customizing a car or truck by removing a few inches horizontally from the top of the vehicle. For example, cutting through the windows and windshield.

Frenching   Customizing a lowrider by installing handles, an antenna, headlights or taillights, or any other part below a vehicle's body to give a smooth look with nothing protruding above the surface.

Pauchuco   A Spanish word for the best lowrider, which means the ultimate in "cool" and is a great compliment.

FURTHER READING

Dunnington, Jacqueline Orsini. *Viva Guadalupe!* Santa Fe, NM: Museum of New Mexico Press, 1997.

Felsen, Henry Gregor, ed. *Here is Your Hobby—Car Customizing.* New York, NY: G. P. Putnam's Sons, 1965.

Lake, E. D. *Lowriders.* Minneapolis, MN: Capstone Press, 1995.

Padilla, Carmella. *Low 'n Slow.* Santa Fe, NM: Museum of New Mexico Press, 1999.

The Visual Dictionary of Cars. New York, NY: Dorling Kindersley, 1992.

Cassette
Gonzalez, Richard, interviewer. *Lowriders.* Los Angeles, CA: Pacifica Radio Archive.

Internet
www.mexonline.com
www.worldbook.com

ABOUT THE AUTHOR

Danny Parr, a freelance writer and former elementary school teacher, lives with her husband in a quiet little Swedish community in central Kansas. When she is not writing, she may be fulfilling business consulting assignments with her husband, jogging, playing the piano or organ, or visiting children and grandchildren. She is the author of the children's book *Jazz from the Inside Out*, a collection of profiles about players who healed their lives through jazz.

PHOTO CREDITS:
Jack Parsons: 2, 6, 9, 10, 14, 17, 18, 21, 24, 27, 29, 30, 34, 36, 39, 42, 45, 49, 50, 52, 55, 56, 58.

INDEX